Last Call

Last Call

Poems

Logan C. Jones

RESOURCE *Publications* · Eugene, Oregon

LAST CALL
Poems

Copyright © 2016 Logan C. Jones. All rights reserved. Except for brief quotations in critical publications or reviews, no part of this book may be reproduced in any manner without prior written permission from the publisher. Write: Permissions, Wipf and Stock Publishers, 199 W. 8th Ave., Suite 3, Eugene, OR 97401.

Resource Publications
An Imprint of Wipf and Stock Publishers
199 W. 8th Ave., Suite 3
Eugene, OR 97401

www.wipfandstock.com

PAPERBACK ISBN 13: 978-1-4982-3322-4
HARDCOVER ISBN 13: 978-1-4982-3324-8

Manufactured in the U.S.A.   01/08/2016

For Sarah and Kate

If you bring forth what is within you,
What you bring forth will save you.

If you do not bring forth what is within you,
What you do not bring forth will destroy you.

> Jesus
> The Gospel of Thomas

Contents

PART I
And He Shall Reign Forever and Ever | 3
The Long Way | 4
The Senior English Poetry Contest | 5
Carrying Your Trash | 7
What Wes Taught Me | 8
When the Whirlwind Comes | 10
The Alchemy of Healing | 11
I See the Ocean | 13
The Coming of Summer | 14
Opening Up | 15
God's Acre | 17
Nothing Less | 19
Asking the Question | 21
Warning Shot | 24
Men's Group | 25
Bringer of Fire | 26
Defining Moments | 28
Kindness | 30
End of October | 33
Homecoming | 34
Pepper | 35
Rain | 37
Summons | 39

Two Moons | 41
After the Lightning Strike | 42

PART II
Home Still Abides | 51
Where Hope Lies | 52
Winter Night | 53
Tender Mercies | 54
Fire Dreams | 56
State Hospital | 57
EMDR | 59
Flight | 60
Pilgrimage | 62
Silver | 63
Fatigue | 66
I Will Hold On | 67
Behind the Chair | 69
Repair | 70
Replacement Gods | 71
The Pathway | 72
$F_g = G\,(m_1 m_2)\,/\,r^2$ | 74
July 3, 1863 | 76
Lord, I Believe . . . | 78
Grail | 80
Visitation | 82
Treadmill | 83
Son of David, Son of Joseph | 85
Sweet Thursday | 87

PART III
Last Call | 91

PART I

And He Shall Reign Forever and Ever

I believe in walking the dog at night
when spirits are alive and dancing.
I believe in music and in good books
that ease the hurting side of pain.
I believe in watching the moon rise
through Carolina pines.
I believe in sitting by a fire,
watching, doing nothing.

I believe in the realness of post-traumatic stress.
I believe in the quiet strength of the
    Blue Ridge Mountains.
I believe the worst thing is not the last thing.
I believe in the Psalms of lament.
I believe in rolling over, pulling up the covers,
    and sleeping in on Saturday mornings.
I believe in the wild danger of poetry.

I don't pretend to know how—
or even what it means—but
I believe He shall reign
               forever and ever.

The Long Way

home
winds through all
the dreams,
and stories,
through all the silences,
and poems
who still believe
in me
when I feel like
I am well nigh on
to lost.

The Senior English Poetry Contest

Good Lord.
The class assignment for high school senior English
was to write a poem.
The poems would be judged by our teachers
and the winning poem would be published

in the school paper.
Big whoop.
No way could I ever write a poem.
I didn't do poetry.
I was too cool,

co-captain of the football team and
we were pretty good that year.
I didn't have time for such nonsense.
So of course I groused and complained,
griped and bitched, bellyached and protested.

An impressive display, but it put no words on paper.
The day before the assignment was due,
my dad finally got tired of my whining.
Out of nowhere he gave me about eight lines,
something about football on Friday nights.

I think it was in iambic pentameter and
it rhymed. That evening I thought
I needed a few more lines.
I called him at his office.
He came to the phone and

out of nowhere gave me four more lines.
Now that was impressive.
I turned in the poem as my own.
And of course it won.
Now I was embarrassed but not

enough to confess.
See, my dad won the senior English poetry contest.
He laughed about it, and was kind of proud.
Actually, though, after all these years,
I realize now I won.

Carrying Your Trash

A man sits in the hotel lobby
reading a book.
No one else is around.
A janitor, about his age, walks by,
says hello and goes into a conference room.
When he comes out,
he is carrying a trash can.
He looks at the man, and says,

    "Any job a person give you,
    you try to be the best at."

He is smiling, doing this one job.
He knows this great truth
and maybe many others.

So . . . how will you live the job given to you?
How will you carry your trash?

What Wes Taught Me

in memory of P. Wesley Aitken

Like a son watching a father
from a distance,
I watched Wes.

He taught me to show up,
that listening to the deep questions matters,
that being steadfast makes a difference.

Wes taught me how to be brave—
    even braver than I ever thought I could be—
by trusting me to make a pastoral visit to a 15-year-old girl
dying of brain cancer
when I did not know what to do,
when I did not know what to say,
when I did not know what to feel,
when I did not know who to be.

Wes taught me how to sail away
from the ease of the shore,
that I could be somebody,
that I could be myself,
just as broken and flawed as he was.

Wes taught me to love graciously
and to be loved gracefully
because that, my friends,
as Wes knew,
       is the only way home.

[P. Wesley Aitken (1924—2014) was the first chaplain and Clinical Pastoral Education supervisor at Duke Hospital, Durham, NC.]

When the Whirlwind Comes

When the whirlwind comes,
    no one escapes.
    All get caught in the shocking winds of sorrow
    and anger and confusion and uncertainty.

The whirlwind says
    love what you have,
    be thankful, be grateful,
    for one day you will be without.
    You will feel all the sadness in the world.
    You will feel the heavy weight of helplessness.
    You will learn about sacrifice.
    You will know of the hard, long road
    and of the hope of home.

When the whirlwind comes,
    you will find your uncommon strength.
    You will discover what it means to be blessed.
    You will know how to yield.

The Alchemy of Healing

Strange work is underfoot
in the darkness,
filled with spells and incantations
and wild hope.
The primal elements are loosed
upon the earth,
upon my soul.

Ancient stories tell
of loosening up,
of unfreezing,
of being tested,
of standing firm,
of rising from ashes.

Through tears
and sorrow
and brokenness,
still searching
for a crumb of hope,
for understanding,
there persists
the longing for blessing
instead of curse.

There remains
the longing for embrace
that eases pain,
that gives
golden courage
to try again
another day,
one more day.

One more time.

I See the Ocean

      and I am sad.

I see the ocean
and understand
that my work
does not matter—
not like how
waves,
wind, and
deep
matter;

not like how
memory,
home, and
mercy

      matter.

The Coming of Summer

The coming of summer is heralded
by storm clouds in the distance,
by sun that warms,
by heat that is both fire and rest,
by sweet breeze that says, wait,
do not hurry;
    go easy on your soul.

It too has its own needs.

Opening Up

He slumps down in the bed,
the IVs are gone;
the catheter has been removed.
The surgery was successful,
the doctor says.

Now he waits for his bowels
to open up,
to release the pent-up
misery of waste.
Then home,

then a time for healing.
But the specter of cancer
hangs in the air.
Is he doomed?
Does he have a second chance?

Or a third?
Do I?
Do any of us?
He looks exhausted.
His eyes are gray.

His wife speaks and
out pours her pent-up fear
and hope as tears smear her make-up.
She opens up
when he cannot, not yet.

I do not even pretend
to know what really heals.

God's Acre

I walk alone among the flat gravestones
in the place called God's Acre.
I read names and dates,
aloud to myself.

Some of the stones are gray
worn by weather,
eroded by far-away grief.
Others are white

not yet torn by the sorrow that will come.
But it will. It always does.
As I walk, it seems
the resting dead speak:

Remember, they say.
Remember who you are.
The cherubim and seraphim
with their red breasts, sharp beaks,

and wild eyes pray and sing
in the cedar trees.
They jump and fly among the graves,
guarding and watching and protecting.

The stones wait to be washed tenderly
and prepared with care for the great Day.
The grass rises to be mowed and caressed.
Flowers will be placed on each grave,

and on Easter morning,
they all will be bathed in sunlight.
From the top of the hill, I watch
four teenagers walk into this sacred space.

Holding hands and touching,
their laughter masks the reality that they, too,
shall one day die,
and maybe rest and wait here.

But laughter should be here too,
here in God's Acre.

Nothing Less

The music came,
    unbidden,
from a place far away.
It was soft, clear, unmistakable—
a hymn from long ago

that sang of Jesus' blood,
his righteousness,
of Christ being a
solid rock.
In the dark times

of the early morning,
I heard the music.
And in my dream,
others began singing softly;
others only mouthed the words.

I tried to sing
but tears filled my eyes
When I awoke
my eyes were wet.
I remember

that twice at Fancy Gap,
a deer spoke to me,
saying,
      You know where hope lies.
So it is true.

My hope,
      my home,
is with God.
Nothing less.

Asking the Question

I.
Jesus said,
If you bring forth what is within you,
what you bring forth will save you.

II.
Before he entered the Grail castle,
Parsifal was told—twice—
to ask,

Whom does the Grail serve?

Asking this question
would heal
the wounded Fisher King.

III.
In my youth, I found myself in the castle
several times
without even knowing it:

I was flooded with emotions at the end
of Godspell when the voice cried out
from the back of the theater,
Prepare ye the way of the Lord.

In my 20s, during my pastoral care training,
I cast out a demon named Legion
in a young woman
in the Emergency Department,
or so they said.

I healed a young girl
with a touch of my hand
and a silent prayer
on the pediatric floor one afternoon,
or so she said.

I wrote some words that
came from a place deep.
They scared me.
So I ran away.

I never asked the question.
I did not know the answer.

IV.
And so it went for 25 years.

V.
Then bruised and battered
by mid-life,
poetry found me.
Words carried me home,
and eased my pain.

I learned I did not
have to answer the question.
Answers are not required;
only asking.

For the Kingdom of God,
like the Grail,
is within.

VI.
Jesus also said,
If you do not bring forth what is within you,
what you do not bring forth will destroy you.

Warning Shot

When your soul is dead,
God is dead.

So whoever you are,
pay attention.
Be careful.
Don't be numb.
Don't go numb.
Stay awake.

Men's Group

We sit in the living room, me and the guys.

Twice a month for two hours, we talk
about our lives, our jobs, and our families.
We tell of our dreams. We speak of our struggles,
our hopes, and sometimes our fears.
We touch on our quiet victories
and our shaming defeats.

These days we talk more about our aging,
not so much about death,
even though we all know it's out there.
During these two hours, there is deep laughter
which brings the soulful healing
that only men can bring to other men.

And there are times of tears, griefs, and frustrations.
But always there is respect and honesty,
as we feebly try, God knows, to be real and say
what we feel
as much as we are able.

I've been with these men for 18 years now—
and I don't do groups—

I would have died without these men,
my brothers.

Bringer of Fire

It's called herpes zoster, shingles.
It's caused by the varicella-zoster virus
which has waited patiently
in the cells of my nervous system
ever since I had chicken pox as a child.
It now arrives on my back and side
with a red, nasty rash
that blisters in anger
and finally crusts over.

Herpes zoster comes with
a subterranean fire in my nerves
to burn away the underbrush
of my life.
The fire brings clarity
even as it continues to explode
like a cluster bomb,
making me howl.

In this fire is my summons
to honor Hephaestus,
the god of fire
who lives in the deep caverns of my soul
with my craftsmanship and art,
so I might see clearly
what I must do
with my life.

From the depths of this fire
I am called upon to hammer out
the shield of Achilles,
the chariot of Apollo, and yes—
to forge even the thunderbolts
of the great Zeus.

Defining Moments

There are a few defining moments
in every person's life.

These moments come unannounced
at unexpected times
in unsuspecting and
crazy-making ways.

These moments come when you stumble
into the abyss of shame,
when a bad choice is made
for unknown reasons
and pain roars.

These moments also come when you take
a simple step towards hope,
when you find your self being
braver, easier, and more merciful
than you ever thought you could be.

These moments bring clarity.
You see who you are becoming, and
who you are meant to be.
The moon shines brighter
when you walk the dog;
music is sweeter;
laughter goes far deeper,
and so do tears.

The sense of thanksgiving
is almost unbearable
when the simple step
sinks into your cells
and you know you are changed—

maybe forever—

and if not forever, then, at least
for now,
and maybe that is enough
to save you.

Kindness

The business was failing,
she says.
I sit on the couch and listen.
I am not sure why
she is telling me this.

The sign said
Going Out of Business.
The hand-woven rugs
were from Turkey,
made by young girls
for their weddings,
with intricate patterns,
exquisite designs,
and rich colors,
now being sold cheap.

She says the father
kept bringing out
all these different rugs
for her to see,
hoping she would buy
at least one.
He told her the story
of coming to this country
to start a new life, but

now that dream
is broken and lost.
Even in his sadness,
the father is patient
and gentle
and kind.

Threads of the rugs
from across the ocean
connect
the young girls
with him and now,
with her.

Across religions and cultures,
time and space
the threads run
together.
They somehow
connect
with me as I
see the tears
in her eyes.

Ah, I know something
about broken
and lost dreams.
Maybe she does too.
Maybe this is why
she is telling me
this story.

As I listen to her,
and, as I have told my story,
I know
dreams may be
lost and broken.

But kindness. . .
kindness lasts

        forever.

End of October

Oak leaves drift down from the trees
covering the lawn,
a precursor to snow. The world turns
inward, away from the sun.
The time of spring and summer is over.

Now is the time of retreat and rest,
but neighbors work like banshees
blowing, raking, and bagging to keep leaves
away from the grass.
But the thrill of a leaf-free lawn is short-lived.

They try so hard. Victory is elusive.
Leaves still fall and
the melanoma still grows no matter
how much blowing, raking, and bagging they do.
Cancer will have its say no matter how

many leaves fall,
no matter where they land.

Homecoming

On the campus the great oaks still welcome
you after all the years.
They have seen many come before
and there will be many after.
They make way for you down the path, past the dorms.
Across the way the domed cathedraled classroom
is washed in sunlight.
It was here
you began the journey to find out
who you were to be.
Little did you know then
that it would be years before you
know as you know now.
The journey ends at home.

Pepper

What do you say to a cat?
Sit? Stay? Good boy?
Do you say, Come here? Fetch?
These words are not right;
they are not enough,
besides they don't work.

Pepper let the girls dress him up in doll clothes,
complete with a bonnet tied neatly under his chin,
and be pushed around in a stroller.
He let the girls put him on leash
and take him for walks in the yard.

He would follow you back home
from your walk around the block,
creeping out from a hiding place in the neighbor's yard.
He would come up the drive way
when you got home from work and fall down,
rolling over so you could rub his tummy
and scratch him behind his ear.

He slept in my chair for hours on end,
leaving behind massive amounts of hair.
He brought home mice and volls,
chipmunks and rabbits, a bird or two
and maybe even a few creatures we didn't know about.

He let himself be loved beyond measure.

What do you say to a cat
who brought joy to one family?

You say,
Thank you.

Rain

It begins with a few drops.
A timpani drum-roll of thunder
floats off in the distance.
Rain doesn't care who
gets wet; the ducks don't care,
neither do the gulls.

Rain will fall on a person
walking on the sidewalk,
a black 735i BMW convertible,
or a red Kia mini-van filled
with screaming children.
It doesn't really matter.

Rain will fall on the landscaping
crew or the yacht tied up
in the marina.
Rain doesn't care.
All it does is wash away
the fatigue, the grime,
the pride, and the anxiety-laden
false self. Hard rain pelts
the skin, soaks the hair and
socks and shoes. It has no need
to care. It does what it is
supposed to do.

Our task is to dry off and
to listen to the gulls;
to live a new life;
to live that life boldly;
and to live it with
    wholehearted gratitude.

Summons

Three hundred Spartan warriors stand
with King Leonidas at Thermopylae.

The NC 26th regiment charges up Cemetery Ridge
for General Lee at Gettysburg.

General Eisenhower orders citizen soldiers
to land and die on Omaha Beach.

No one from the 7th Air Calvary is left behind
at Ia Drang, just as Colonel Moore promised

* * * * * *.

The battles I face are small.
I fight about budgets and space,
FTEs and stipend dollars,
things of import
but really of no matter
in the end.

* * * * * *

Could I stand with Leonidas
and not falter?

Could I be that brave?

Would I have enough courage
to stand tall with my brothers?

Would my heart be strong enough
so not to fall away?

Could I endure what would be asked of me
with honor?

* * * * * *

I do not know the answers.

I simply wonder where my king
will summons me,
what he will call forth from me,
and if I will be able to follow.

Two Moons

In a dream—I think—I see two moons.
I am standing in the driveway of the house
where I grew up.
A young man is with me.
He is in his 20s, a life ahead of him.

Off in the east, a full moon shines,
its light reflecting off the clouds.
Then to the south, just a little higher in the sky,
there is another moon,
even fuller, even brighter.

I am not sure what this dream means,
but somehow I know
two moons will show me
my path.
Maybe She always has.

After the Lightning Strike

1.
If one more person says,
"Well, at least you all got out safely,"
or "I'm glad no one was hurt,"
or "All your belongings can be replaced,"
or "You will get a new house of out this,"

I will turn and walk away,
raging inside because they have no idea
what it was like that night,
that night when the untold Fury rained
down on us all,
that night when flames screamed
and smoke rolled out of windows,
that night when we lost almost
everything,
that night when we were marked
                                      forever.

2.
The imprint of that lightning bolt remains inside of me:

The great storms of summer move over the land, bringing the sweet sound of rain along with wind, flashes of light, and sounds of thunder as we turn out the lights. I love to sleep when it is raining.

Then . . . a bomb explodes over our heads. The house shakes and groans. The crack and power of the Destroyer is upon us. There is a shower of flaming plaster onto the bed . . . terror and screams fill the dark night. The bed is on fire and there is fire on the wall. Jesus. Our house is burning . . . Kelli's arm has been burned. She screams for Katie to get the dog and get out. I grab a pillow from the floor and try to beat out the flames on the bed. There is no light, only fire. I cannot find my glasses. The picture on the wall has been blown off. I cannot see. I keep beating the fire. Jesus. Kelli calls 911 and runs outside, safe with Katie. I try to fight the fire but it is too much. It roars up from underneath the mattress and up the wall, angry. The room takes on an eerie glow. There is nothing I can do. I think about running into the kitchen to get the fire extinguisher but the smoke, all the smoke, is beginning to fill the house. It rolls up the hallway into the den and kitchen. I am helpless. I am powerless to stop it.

I run outside. Kelli and Katie are at Alice's house. It is raining like crazy. The thunder and lightning will not stop and our house is burning and there is nothing I can do. I run to the street, screaming for the firefighters, cursing and yelling out of fear, shock, and helplessness. Where are they? What is taking so long? Don't they know we need help? Jesus. Why don't they come?

There is nothing I can do but watch as the flames race up into the night sky. The rain does nothing. The fire roars out of the windows and

through the roof. I stand there, in the rain, in
my boxers, not being able to see, and seeing all
of our possessions, our home, burn.

We are losing everything, everything.

3.
The early morning hours bring shock and
numbness, not knowing what to do
and there is so much to do.
Everything is dulled and a borrowed
pair of glasses brings a headache to go along
with the heartache. EMTs check Kelli's
arm and ask about chest pains and smoke
inhalation. Katie sits on the couch holding
our dog.

It breaks my heart to see her trying to be so
strong. We have to call Sarah in Savannah
to tell her.

A neighbor returns from WalMart with clothes
for us . . . underwear, shorts, shirts, shoes.
At least I now have something to wear beside
my wet boxers and a blanket. Other neighbors
come to sit with us while we wait for the
firefighters to finish. Someone said there were
> six fire trucks,
> 26 firefighters,
> two ambulances,
> two fire department SUVs,
> and a police car.

I am in a daze, hollowed out
by the fury and fear.
It is no good to go to all the "what ifs . . ."
There are too many.

So finally in the darkness of the early

morning, the captain says we can
go through our home.

Jesus Christ.

The smell. I will never forget that smell
of destruction. The house is black inside, no
lights, only flashlights held by the firefighters
guiding us over burned debris of our lives.

Our home is hurt beyond belief.

Our bedroom is scorched, nothing is left. All
the furniture, clothes, sheet rock, insulation
burned beyond recognition and pitched outside.
The fire ripped through the attic leaving a
gaping wound in the roof.

Jesus.

I can barely stand to see it. Comprehension
eludes me. The firefighters moved all of
Sarah's furniture into the middle of her room
and covered it with a plastic tarp to try and
protect it. Katie's room is a mess of blackened
soot.

God, I wish I had thought to close doors before I
ran out, but I did not.
I did the best I could.

The wallpaper in the hallway is seared off, the
thermostat melted, and goddamned black soot
covers the den, kitchen, living room . . .

Everything is touched, all ruined. Am I?

Will I be able to be repaired?

After this?

Beyond this?

4.
The light of dawn brings kindness—
and hidden tears.

I doze for maybe an hour. I am
still numb, stricken by the largeness
of the fire, the disaster, the trauma.

My soul hurts.

Sarah cries when we tell her. She is coming
home. I need to see her.

Friends and neighbors come bringing
food, bringing awkward gifts, bringing
themselves, bringing hope.

We are loved and cared for
beyond measure,

                      beyond fire.

5.
Sleep, if it comes, is fleeting
and fitful. I cannot turn my mind
off nor my heart. I hear Kelli's
screams. I feel the fear. I see
the flames howl up the wall,
hissing at me.
I feel my helplessness. I stand
at the top of the driveway
in the cold rain,

                      shaking.

The magnitude of what lies before us
is overwhelming. We have to see
what is salvageable.
I hope I am.
We have to see about an inventory
of our things, our clothes,
our furniture, our books,
our pictures, our dishes,

                                      our lives.

I am depleted. I am exhausted.
I am running on

                                      empty.

6.
The demolition process is brutal.
Dumpsters are filled up over
and over again with chairs, sweaters,
shirts, pants, lamps, desks, rugs,
t-shirts, cleaning supplies, socks, towels,
shampoo and soap, cabinets, vacuum cleaner,
pottery, end tables, dressers, sheets, blankets,
quilts, underwear, pajamas, CDs and
DVDs, mattresses, sinks, toilets, books, sofas,
tables, pots and pans, stereos, dishes, more
books, glasses, sheet rock, insulation,
flooring, stove, rocking chairs, plumbing,
wiring, secretary, antique buffet, mirrors, shoes,
coats, pictures, bookcases, tupperware,
carpet, ceiling fans, light fixtures, bed frames,
and more books. All and more tossed away
quickly and quietly.
We will have to be keepers
of the stories now.

7.
Things I have learned so far:

Trauma really sucks.
I do not like shopping.
I miss my books.
I can find ways to step up.
I have a limited amount of energy.
I can be braver than I thought.
I worry too much about money.
Home is an anchor.
I do not have the words to say how deeply I
        love my wife and my daughters.

I can live in gratitude.

8.
We lost a lot.

I found even more.

PART II

Home Still Abides

A fire destroyed our house
but not our home.

We lost almost everything
but not each other.

Many things were unsalvageable
but not my gratitude.

I thought it would break me
but it did not.

Our house is being rebuilt
but our home still

                      abides.

Where Hope Lies

I walk up the road
towards the Blue Ridge Parkway.
It is almost dusk.
The clouds are red and far away.
From the woods at the bend
a deer runs towards me.
I stop, startled and not moving.
She looks at me,
lifts one leg.
She says,
You know what to do.
You know where hope lies.
You know who to be.

That is enough.

Winter Night

The fire leaps for joy
and prays the Psalms.
I sink into its warmth.
Wrapped in dreams,
I rest from the sharp teeth of the cold.
I am surrounded
by laughter,
and find hope
in the caress of
its sweet,
    life-giving
mercy.
There is no hurry now.
There is nothing to do.
Sit. Wait.
Listen. Be still.
Let darkness come.
I am not afraid.
Not anymore.

This is eternal. Life.

Tender Mercies

How does it happen,
this mystery of mercy?
How does it work?

What really happens when undeserved,
unmerited, and unearned
mercy touches the heart?

What happens when mercy is
given freely, without rancor
and without judgment?

Ah, like poetry, mercy is dangerous
because once received
the change is forever.

I do not know how or why
mercy works. I only know
that if the head

will not bow,
then the heart
will not open,

and if the heart
will not open,
then it will never heal.

Only when the heart
is healed may mercy
be given to the deep need

in someone else.

Fire Dreams

Shingles brought me to my knees.
My nerves were on fire. I howled
as I wrote my dissertation.

Our house burned after a lightning strike.
That night I saw the Destroyer
in the hiss and anger of the fire.

Now when I dream of fire—
the house does not burn,
the flames do not race up the wall,

the furniture is left without damage.
There is no smell and no awful
black soot on everything.

I was afraid I was ruined
and beyond repair.
My dreams tell me that

maybe, just maybe,
I am not.

State Hospital

The class was called Advanced Abnormal Psychology.
The classroom was the state mental hospital
about two hours away from campus
where we watched, listened, and learned about mental illness.
Our first assignment was to befriend a patient
on the locked adult male ward.
That seemed easy enough.
The attendant in a white uniform with the huge key ring
opened the heavy door.
He had a weird little smile on his face
as the door slammed behind us.

Ronnie was looking out the window.
He was young, dressed nicely.
He had not been beaten down
by institutionalization at that point.
I chose to befriend him. He looked safe.
He told me he was waiting
for his parents to come and pick him up.
He could not understand why they were late.
He talked some about the fire,
how all the snakes kept crawling on his stomach.
He kept looking out the window.
I jumped up and left.

On the adult locked female ward,
the music therapist had all the patients
sit around in a circle among the staff.
A middle-aged woman with heavy makeup and
red, off-centered lipstick kept eyeing me.
I did not want to make eye contact,
but she had me in her sights.
While the therapist played her guitar and sang,
she came over, plopped in my lap, and
put her arms around me.
She wanted to know if I was married.
As I squirmed, she kissed me on the cheek,
marking me with her lipstick.
I stand up, forcing her off my lap.
I moved to the other side of the room
trying to get away but she kept following.

She still follows me sometimes.
I wish I could have been kinder
to her and Ronnie,
but I was too scared.

EMDR

Listen.
Close your eyes.
Go deep.
Deeper.
Stay with the images.

Listen to both sides.
Do not be afraid
of both sides.
Both are true.

Listen to both sides.
Do not be afraid
of the questions.
Trust both sides.

Trust the transformation
of your frozen heart.
Stories melt the ice.
Listen for the melting.
Poetry rekindles the fire.
There is no other way.

Flight

I.
In the dark time of winter
I was lost,
but did not know it.
I was empty,
but did not feel it.

I was numb—
un-knowing and un-feeling,
I could not find my way.
The sword of Herod
swung wildly,
seeking to slaughter.
I did not know where to go.
I only knew
that if I stayed,
I would die.

II.
I took flight to Egypt,
a place of wilderness,
    exile,
        and mystery,
a place unvisited for so long.

Darkness is the time
for searching for home.
Winter is the time
of seeking rest.
The way home is through Egypt
because Egypt is
also a place of healing.

III.
On the way,
an angel
of the Lord appeared
and said,
Do not be afraid.
I will help you feel.
I will hear your story.
I will help you go home.

Pilgrimage

Mary Oliver made me cry
when she said: one day
you finally knew what you
had to do—save the only
life you could save.

David Whyte stunned me
when he said: something
new was being written
in the ashes of my life.

Stanley Kunitz left me without words
when he said: live in
the layers, not the litter.

That is enough.
I do not need to know
the Where, or the How,
or even the When. I only
have to trust doing what I
have to do, believe in the
newness of my life, and
live gracefully in the layers.

God have mercy on my soul.

Silver

1.
We found him on the deck, stretched out.
It looked like he was asleep but no.
The cat was dead,
deader than a doornail.
He had not been sick and

there were no signs of distress,
only a little blood at the corner of his mouth.
Silver was gone.
He up and died on us.
We put him a box.

Burial would be in the morning.
Thunderstorms were moving into the area
and we went to bed.
We were almost asleep
when the lightning bolt hit the house.

We all got out with just our pajamas;
everything else was destroyed.
I tried to put out the fire on the mattress
but it was too much.
I finally ran out.

I have wondered at times
during this past year if Silver had been alive
would I have run down to the basement to get him.
I knew Kelli, Kate and the dog were safe.
Probably so. Maybe.

That would not have been very smart,
But he was gone.
Now I am here, grateful,
mystified by this cat who died
the night our house burned.

2.
        (by Kelli Walker-Jones)
That cat would nip at my heels every time
I tried to bound up the stairs.

Rub me, notice me, feed me.

He was not content to hope,
He took action and communicated clearly.
Of all the cats I have ever had,
he was my least favorite
and perhaps the most beautiful.

His eyes illuminated with green light,
piercing, just like the claws at my heels.
In the midst of a rub, for no good reason,
he would bite my hand.
He did bite the hand that fed him.

I fed him anyway.

But his gracefulness at the end
turned my feelings upside down.
How did he know?

His heart-friend, Sarah, would be relieved
to know he did not suffer or fear.
His nemesis, Logan, would not go downstairs
to look for him,
keeping Logan safe for his family.
And here I sit, almost one year later,
sobbing for that cat.
We move back in soon,
but he will not be there.

Fatigue

Here is the change
required:

Do not fight now;
let whatever comes as it comes;
trust the turning;
shed the resistance;
listen to your life;
be open to Joy and Sadness;
let both be part of your life.

The redemption of fatigue
is found in Praise,
in giving Thanks,
in living in Gratitude,
in welcoming my ancient
brothers and sisters.

I Will Hold On

I will hold on
to the mercy of imagination
rather than
the theological hacksaws
of a dried up faith.
I will hold on
to the mercy of laughter
rather than
the cheap words
of a lost institution.
I will hold on
to the mercy of sunset
rather than
the ineptness
of the imperial academy.

I will trust the waves
to wash away my sin,
not some shriveled-up words
that have given up
their meaning.
I will trust the pelicans
to speak truth,
not fearful old men
who have no boldness.
I will trust the setting of the sun
to show me how
my life should set—

easy, colorful,
with a hint of sadness,
a clapping of hands.

Behind the Chair

As a young boy, I learned to play
by myself behind the chair in the living room.
My army trucks kept me company
and gave me hours of fun.
I learned to be hidden,
to stay out of the way.
I learned that my needs did not matter,
that my needs were not important.
I learned not to bother anyone.
Behind the chair I was safe.
    There I was alone.
    There I was lonely.
Years later, I still know how to be invisible.
But now I want something different.
I want to find the courage
to come out from behind the chair.

Repair

The hole is fixed, the surgeon said.
You will be sore for several days and
there will be some bruising.
Other than that, you will be fine.
The repair will hold.

Can I say that about
my relationship with her?

It is slowly being fixed.
I feel it. It is being healed.
I don't know if the soreness and
the bruising will ever go away.
No matter.

The repair will hold.

Replacement Gods

The God beyond God is now in hiding.
So we are left—sadly—with worshiping
our replacement gods:
like the powerful god named Science
and the dark god, Technology.
We pay homage to the gods
called Materialism, Progress, and Patriotism.
We clamor for the elusive gods called Health and Youth.
We bow down to Entertainment.
We pay our tributes to the great and almighty god,
    the Free Market.
But still.
We are empty and cold.
Maybe when we are empty enough and cold enough
we will search again for God.

The Pathway

I have dreamed about it.
I have seen it in my sleep.

Hell, I think I've walked on it—
haltingly and carefully and fearfully—
in my youth a time or two,
but I did not know it then.

I thought I had to travel
the path alone,
by myself—
solitary, isolated, and invisible.

But, somehow and someway,
on the pathway
I began to see
my many different selves,
waiting to be welcomed
and forgiven.

I saw the young boy, playing behind the chair;
the angry adolescent, unable to give voice,
the cocky athlete, exuding confidence and bravado;
the quiet adult, confused by poetry;
the lost son without a father;
the man struggling at midlife
who knows of shame and fear,
trying to learn about courage.

I long to find my way back to the Castle
even when I am not sure of the way.

I long to return to the Castle
to ask the Question

and to offer my sacrifice.

$$F_g = G\,(m_1 m_2)\,/\,r^2$$

(Gravity)

Home is an emotional force defined
by the gravitational pull of
mother, father, furniture, location, smell,
shadow, and mystery.
Home is constellated
by a universal longing born in us.
We carry this longing
all of our lives to the grave and beyond,
for good and ill.

Home is defined by a restlessness
of attraction and repulsion
as the emotional mass of the particles of home
exert their power over us.

Some of us find everything we need at home
and so choose to stay.
Others are trapped,
pulled into the black hole of home
where there is no escape, where no light gets out,
where the soul is swallowed up
slowly and quietly, bit by bit,
until all that is left is a dull ache that has no name.

Some of us are expelled, sent into exile,
hurling into the outer reaches.
Others explode in leaving
and burn brightly in an arc
against the darkened sky.

Yet some of us are blessed to leave,
to find our way to another home,
knowing we can always return.
To find home is to surrender
to gravity and
belonging.

July 3, 1863

I was seventeen in 1863,
and been to hell and back for Robert E. Lee.
I was fighting with the North Carolina Twenty-Sixth.
We knew we could never be whipped.

We clashed at Gettysburg that hot July day.
We waited in the woods and took time to pray.
Many were already lost and Stonewall was gone.
I wondered if I would ever see another sunrise at dawn.

We moved across the field, slowly at first.
We marched to our glory as our throats burned with thirst.
Great long lines of men, between us no room.
We stayed steady as we marched to our doom.

Cannon rained upon us and so many fell.
So many dying among the screams and the Rebel Yell.
There was smoke, cries, rivers of blood, and tears.
I now knew that I had no more years.

We reached the highest point at the wall.
Guns exploded, yet we stood tall.
We got so close and yet so far.
Did the guns ever stop? Did our cries reach the stars?

Tell my mama it didn't hurt.
Tell my brother how hard I tried.
Tell my daddy I was brave.
Tell them it was in Pickett's Charge where I died.

Lord, I Believe . . .

I believe in God the Father,
    maker of Heaven and Earth.

I believe in God the Mother,
    giver of life and home.

I believe in God the Grandfather,
    teacher of laughter and wisdom.

I believe in God the Grandmother,
    holder of tantrum and anger.

I believe in God the Brother,
    watcher of my back.

I believe in God the Sister,
    keeper of family lore.

I believe in God the Son,
    my oldest friend and fiercest foe.

I believe in God the Daughter,
> sustainer of courage and journey.

I believe in you,
> the great love of my life.

And I believe in me.

Help Thou my unbelief.

Grail

There were whispers at recess:
Tommy has the picture—
Yes, he really has it this time—
    Don't tell anyone—
    Meet at the tobacco barn behind
Sonny's house after school—
Make sure no one sees you.

The sweet smell of cured tobacco
saturates the barn. Empty whiskey bottles
are scattered about, left by
    the grandfathers who tended
    the fires through the night.
Now in the late afternoon,
another fire waits.

The picture has been folded and refolded
many times. It is grainy and faded.
It needs to be handled
    with great care. Craig opens it.
    We strain like a pack of young pups
to see. Sixth grade boys are driven
by forces we do not understand.

And there She is:

white breasts, dark pubic hair,
hips that have no end to the curves,
long black hair, gentle shoulders,
    and a killer smile.
    Of course, we do not spend any time
looking at her smile.
We are without words.

Our bravado belies our fear.
Our stirrings run alongside of our sense
of being bad, that we should not be looking.
    This mysterious, other-worldly
    goddess is beyond us.
We leave the tobacco barn
with a deep unsayable hope

that has never left.

Visitation

A middle-aged woman shows up unannounced,
unexpectedly,
in my dream.
She sits on the edge of the bed
but does not speak.
Somehow I know she loves me,
accepts me,
forgives me.
There is nothing else I need to know.

Treadmill

The need to be well runs deep
as we work out at the wellness center.
We come in all shapes and sizes—
the young alpha males ripped with razor sharp
edges and a few tattoos, the middle-aged men
and women, mostly fat and doughy,
a few thin and wiry even to anorexic,
and our great elders with their canes,
walkers, and oxygen tanks.

The fashion sense is stunning—
old men in knee-high black socks
with Rockport walking shoes,
middle-aged men in cargo shorts,
headbands around the bald heads,
new hip clothes with bright neon shoes,
old tank tops, t-shirts, gym shorts from the 70s,
yoga pants, even tote bags and purses guarded
closely by the elderly women.

We choose our workout routines—
stretching to warm up, walking on the treadmills,
climbing hills on the elliptical machines,
riding the stationary bikes, rowing on,
of course, the rowing machines, swimming laps,
lifting the free weights watching ourselves in the mirror,
spin classes, TRX classes, yoga,
or using the high-tech weight machines.

We all wish to escape our human fate,
harboring the unspoken, secret thought—
    Maybe I will be the one.
But no matter how many miles
walked, ran, swam, cycled, or rowed,
no matter how many hills climbed,
or how much weight lifted,
or how many classes taken,
we will all die.

None of us will get out alive—
there are no exemptions,
no exceptions. Not one.
Be grateful.

Son of David, Son of Joseph

A Prayer

Thou art the pioneer and perfecter of my faith.
Thou art my Alpha and Omega.
Thou art the Resurrection and the Life.
Why, then, O Lord of my heart,
am I afraid of Thee?

Why art Thou far off and hidden from me
in my time of need?
Wilt Thou answer if I cry out?
Or wilt Thou turn and be silent?
I am afraid of both.

I beseech Thee, O Lord of my fathers,
to be gentle with me these days.
I seek something I am unable to name.
Find it in Thy mercy to show me.
Pour out Thy spirit upon me, Thy servant,

for I am broken, wandering, and bewildered.
Show me the path
which Thou wouldst have me travel.
Guide me, O Lord, with Thy mercy and
    forgiveness.

Thou hast given me joy undeserved
and likewise sorrow.
Help me to remember
that Thou art in both;
indeed that Thou art both.

Remember me, O Lord.
Be Thou the Christ to me as Thou need to be.
Be gracious unto me, sweet Jesus.
Be Thou my hope.
Be Thou my vision.

Sweet Thursday

> *For Kelli*
> *with apologies to John Steinbeck*

Like Doc, I too know something
about the deep voice of lonesome
and the crazy hunger that prowls
in the dark hours.
I too know something
about paralysis and discontent
and seeking for something,
anything,
that will melt the hard
edges of my heart.

A seer told Doc long ago
that nothing big can be done without—
    without love.
He left Doc to go help the sun go down.
The sun needed him, he said, and
he walked towards the west.
I did not understand what he meant
but I knew it was true.

Like Doc, I know something
about how One Woman
brings whole-ness and
alive-ness into my bewildering life.
Now in the middle years of
the sweet days with Kelli,
she brings the music of heaven,
the thrill of chocolate chips cookies,
and, as I sleep beside her, elusive
knowledge of great peace, gratitude,
and astonishment.

While she would say it is not so,
she brings to me courage to embrace
the simplicity of who I am
                            and my changing.

PART III

Last Call

Last call at the neighborhood bar gives
you time to get that final shot of bourbon.

Last call at the baseball game means
there is time for one more $9 can of warm beer.

But in life, last call often comes without warning.
It just happens. Time runs out.

Things shut down; doors close;
lights turn off. It's over.

Yet—God's last call for us is different.
The spigot of grace remains wide open.

Forgiveness never runs out.
Mercy is never-ending, sweet and refreshing.

God's last call is YES.
Always YES. Always.

www.ingramcontent.com/pod-product-compliance
Lightning Source LLC
Chambersburg PA
CBHW070321100426
42743CB00011B/2512